The Happy Lines Family
Halloween Animals
Coloring and Activity Book

Copyright © 2023 C. & L.& H. Lopez Espina

Published by The Little Book Farmers Happy Lines Family

Published in the United States of America

All rights reserved. No part of this publication can be reproduced, copied, transmitted, stored, or recorded in any manner whatsoever without written permission from the copyright owners. Commercial resale in any form is strictly prohibited.

To request permission, contact Little Book Farmers/ *The Happy Lines Family* at:

https://littlebookfarmers.com/contact-us/

Written and Edited by: C. & L. & H. Lopez Espina
Illustrated by: L. Lopez Espina

ISBN: 978-1-962850-01-8

Name _____ Date _____

My Halloween Book

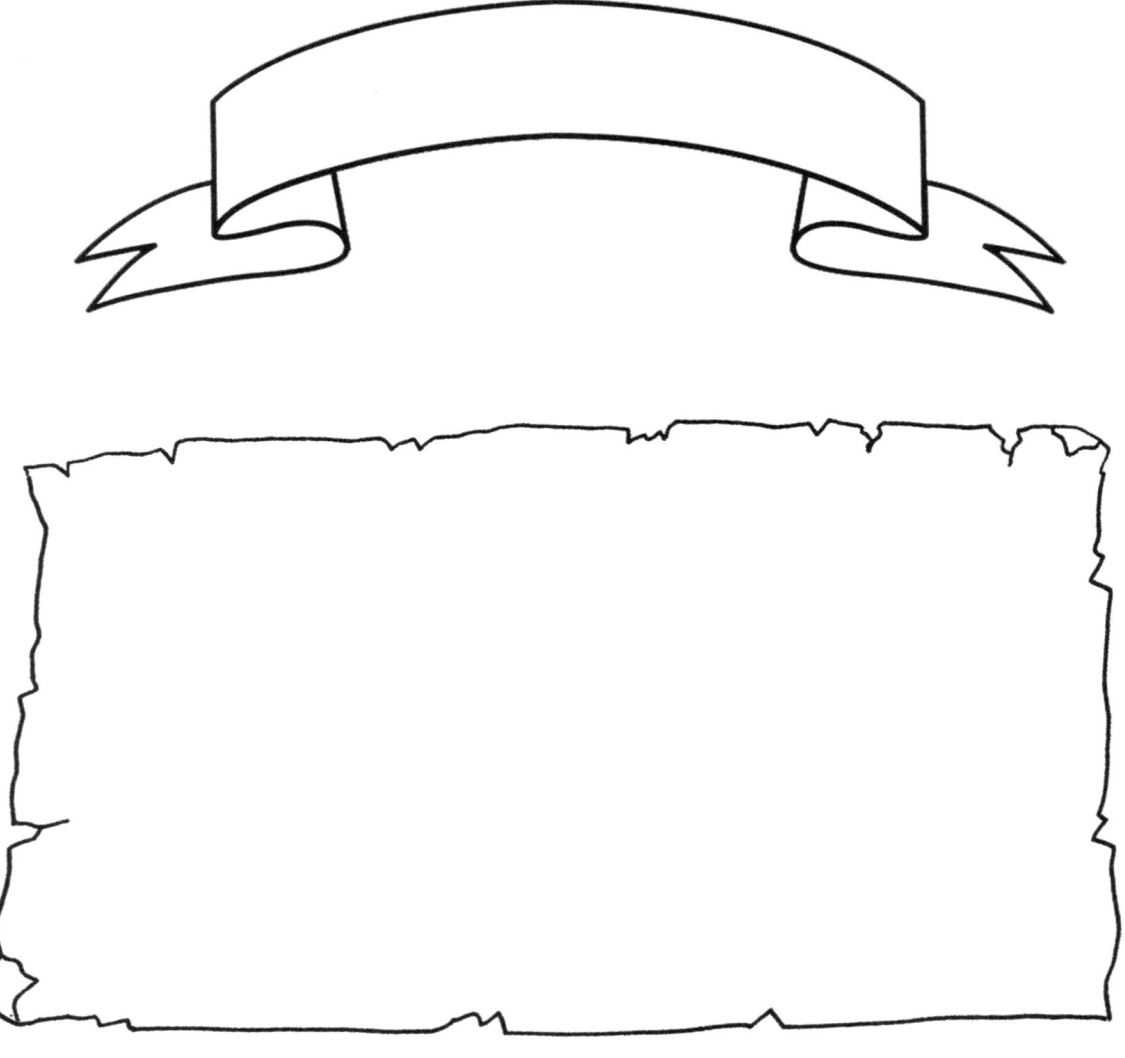

My Halloween Coloring Book

This book belongs to:

Acorn

We *acorns* grow into **oak trees**. We begin to grow when oak trees are about 20 to 50 years old. Also, squirrels can carry about eight of us in their cheek pouches.

Sometimes a good book can make you a little *nutty!*

Alien

Do you know that *you* would be considered an alien to to any life form existing on another planet?

Anglerfish

Only we female **anglerfish** are **bioluminescent** (which means glow). The males are very small, and when they find their true love, they *literally* stay attached to one of us for life, we'll actually share the same bloodstream eventually! Also, many people didn't know that we can swim close to the ocean surface, although we never stay for long. We like to lay half-tucked into the moist ocean floor sand in what's known as the **midnight zone** of the ocean, about a whole mile deep.

The Halloween Folding Game Part 1

The **Halloween Folding Game** is a fun two-to-three player game. You will need a sheet of paper and a pen or pencil. You can use crayons or colored pencils too.

How to play:

1. Fold a piece of paper into three equal sections just like you would fold a letter into an envelope. Number each folded segment: 1. for the head, 2. for the neck and body, and 3. for the legs and feet.

2. **The first player** draws the head of the Halloween creature on fold 1. When finished, fold the paper inward under segment three. Next, draw two small marks on segment 2. to show where the neck and body will continue. Make sure no one can see your drawing!

3. **The next player** draws the neck and body on segment 2. using the marks as a starting point. Then turn the paper over to section 3. and mark where the legs and feet begin. Pass it to the next player without letting anyone see what has been drawn.

4. **The last player** draws the legs and feet on segment 3. Then all together open up the folded paper to reveal a hilarious Halloween creature!

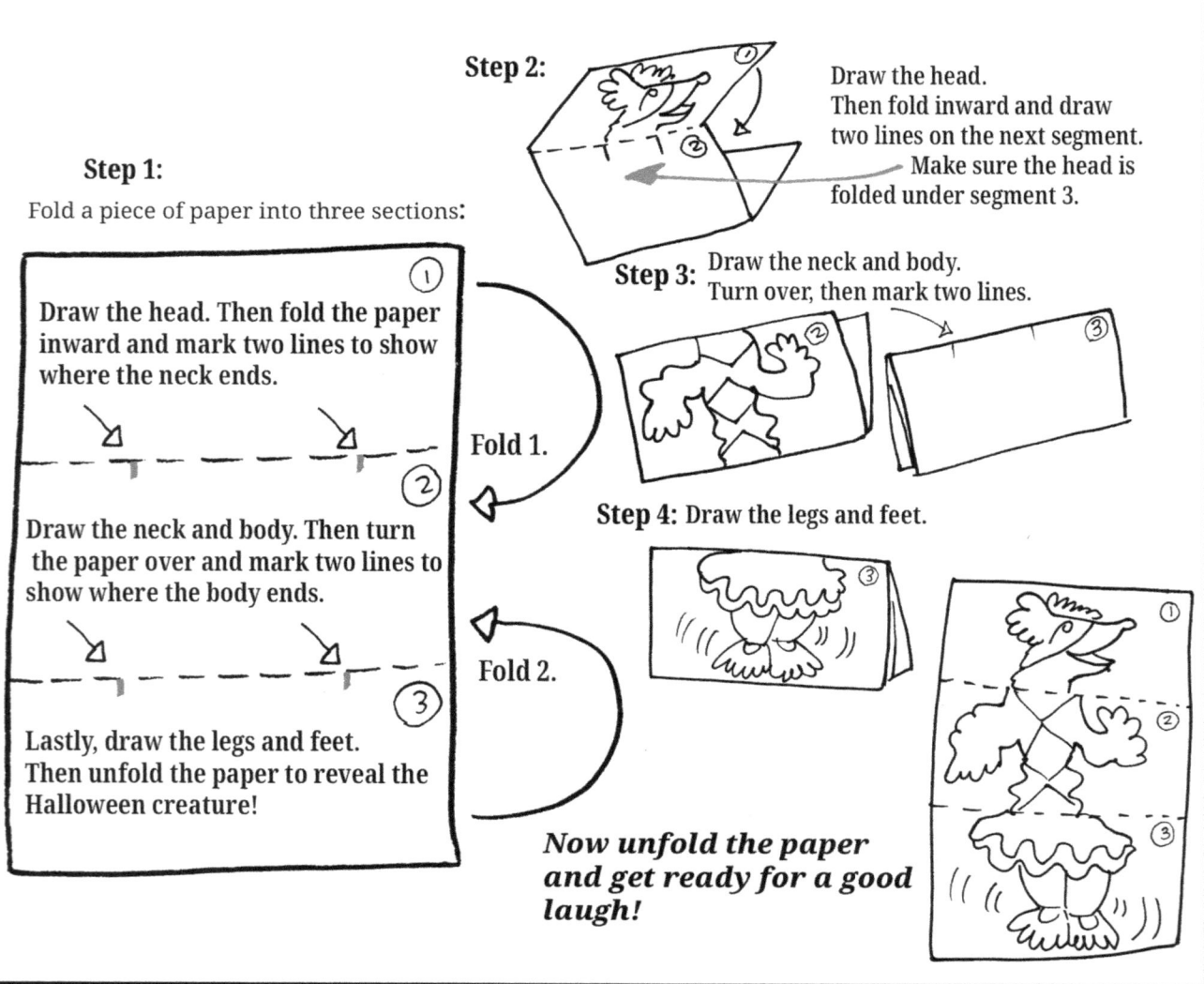

Now unfold the paper and get ready for a good laugh!

1.

2.

3.

1.

2.

3.

1.

2.

3.

1.

2.

3.

The Halloween Folding Game Part 2:
The Halloween Mix-Match Game

Once you have played **The Halloween Folding Game Part 1**, you can try **The Halloween Mix-Match Game**. You will need to have three or more completed Halloween creatures, and a pair of scissors.

1. Cut along each of the folds.

2. Lay all the pieces face down on a large surface (table, floor, etc.) and mix them up.

3. Each player chooses three pieces to begin making new creatures. But, this time, they may all turn out to be heads or feet. You can keep playing until someone gets a complete creature.

4. You can also have lots of fun putting together different combinations to find the funniest creatures of all.

5. Use your imagination. Don't forget that you can always invent new games. The possibilities are endless!

You can save all of your drawings in an envelope to play later.
The more drawings you save up, the funnier the game will become!

A little history about Tic-Tac-Toe:

Versions of the game Tic-Tac-Toe can be traced back to ancient times.

The Egyptians played a version with rocks and shells.

The Romans used pebbles in a game called, "Terni Lapilli," meaning three-pebbles-at-a-time.

A Native American version of the game is called, "Picaria".

In China, Tic-Tac-Toe is called "Jǐng Zì Qí" or "Quān Quān Chā Chā".

"Marupeke" is the Japanese name for a version of Tic-Tac-Toe.

In the United Kingdom, the Republic of Ireland, New Zealand, Australia, parts of Africa, and India, Tic-Tac-Toe is known as "Noughts/Naughts and Crosses".

In Spanish-speaking countries, it's known as, "Tres en Raya," and "Totito".

You can do some research on your own to find out more, and to learn how to play fun versions of the game from around the world and long ago.

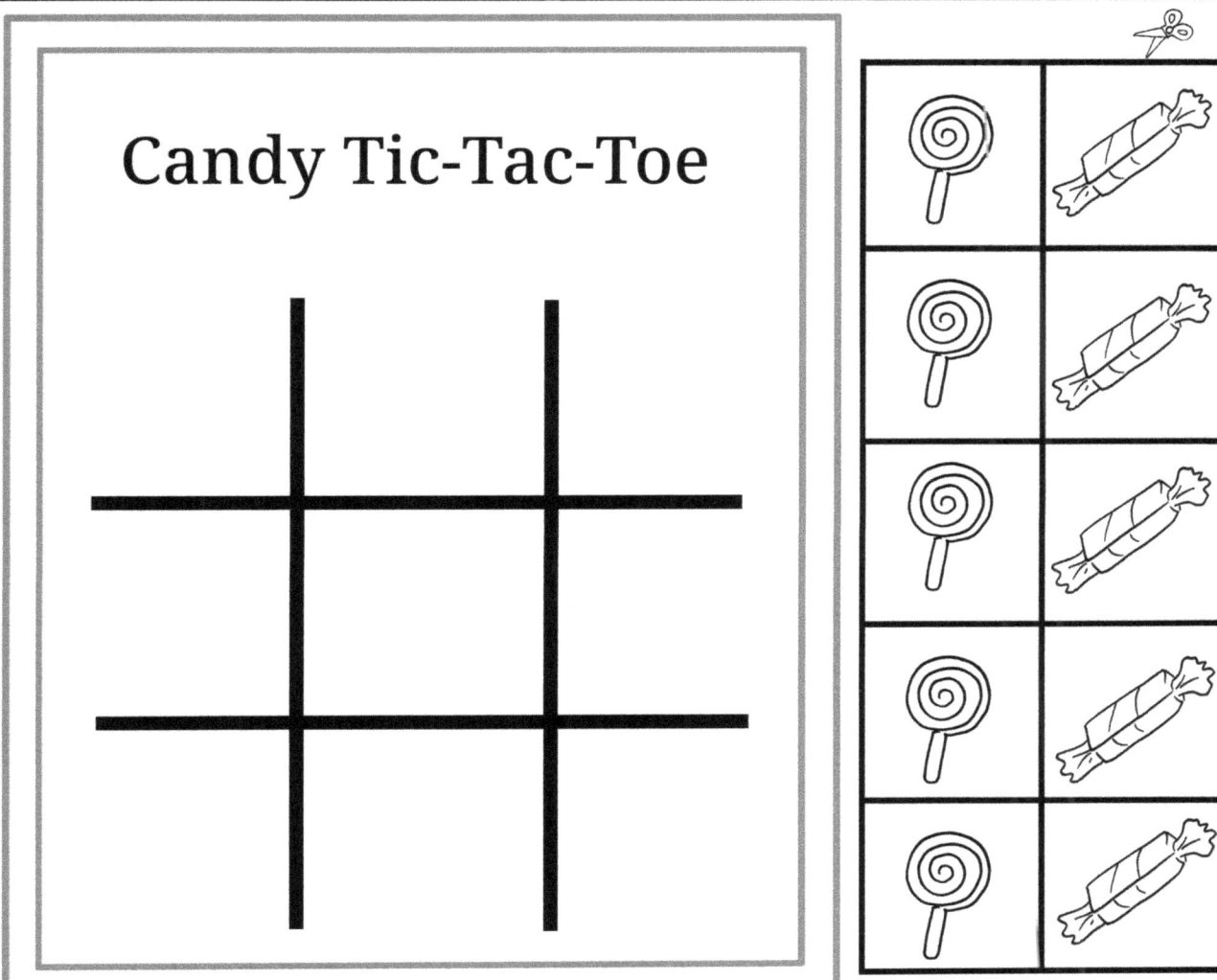

Candy Tic-Tac-Toe

Candy Tic-Tac-Toe is a deliciously fun two-player game. You can use some of your real Halloween candy instead of the cut-out candies for an *extra sweet* game (but ask your parents first)!

How to play:

1. Each player gets a set of five like pieces.

2. The youngest player goes first, placing one of their pieces on any square.

3. Each person gets one turn at a time until someone wins by getting three pieces in a row.

4. In some cases, no one gets three in a row. That's called a draw. Have fun!

Instructions:

1. Color the page however you like.

2. Carefully cut out the pieces.

3. You can laminate the pieces with packing tape to make them last longer.

4. Decorate an envelope to store the game board and pieces. If you don't have one,

you can make one by stapling, or taping two pieces of paper together.

Halloween Word Search:

Tip: Search row by row, up, down, backward, and diagonally (means across). Never give up, you will find them all!

B	A	T	Y	Z	W	O	L	F	C	H	S
O	I	A	A	S	L	I	M	E	H	T	T
O	H	C	H	O	U	F	P	A	E	G	A
G	J	C	O	S	T	U	M	E	S	L	R
E	W	Y	W	R	X	N	W	E	S	Z	R
F	A	L	L	A	Q	S	H	A	P	P	Y
T	R	I	C	K	O	R	T	R	E	A	T
C	S	H	A	L	L	O	W	E	E	N	O
A	H	Z	T	L	O	L	L	I	P	O	P
N	A	B	R	O	O	M	S	T	I	C	K
D	R	P	U	M	P	K	I	N	R	A	T
Y	E	M	U	M	M	Y	B	M	O	O	N

1. Halloween
2. Bat
3. Cat
4. Owl
5. Wolf
6. Trick Or Treat
7. Rat
8. Happy
9. Candy
10. Mummy
11. Slime
12. Boo
13. Moon
14. Lollipop
15. Star
16. Fun
17. Broomstick
18. Costumes
19. Fall
20. Pumpkin
21. Sweet
22. Share

Bats

Did you know people build us **"bat houses"** on the side of their homes to help keep mosquitoes and flies away? Yes, we bats are a natural pest control that doesn't harm our earth! On the contrary, **we are very helpful in many ways**. Many insects that are pests to humans, happen to be important and delicious meals for us. They are also food for birds, lizards, frogs, and many other animal friends that we share the planet with. Like many bees, bugs, rodents, and birds, we are very important **pollinators** (pollinators carry pollen from one plant to another, which leads to the creation of new plants). You can call pollinators the cupids of the plant world. Did I mention that we are the only mammals that can fly?What can I say, ***We bats are incredibly useful and necessary. Simply amazing!***

Batty Halloween Jokes

What is the best sport to play on Halloween?

A: Baseball. Because every candy is a **Home Run**!

Write your own *batty* Halloween joke here:

_____

_____

_____

_____

_____

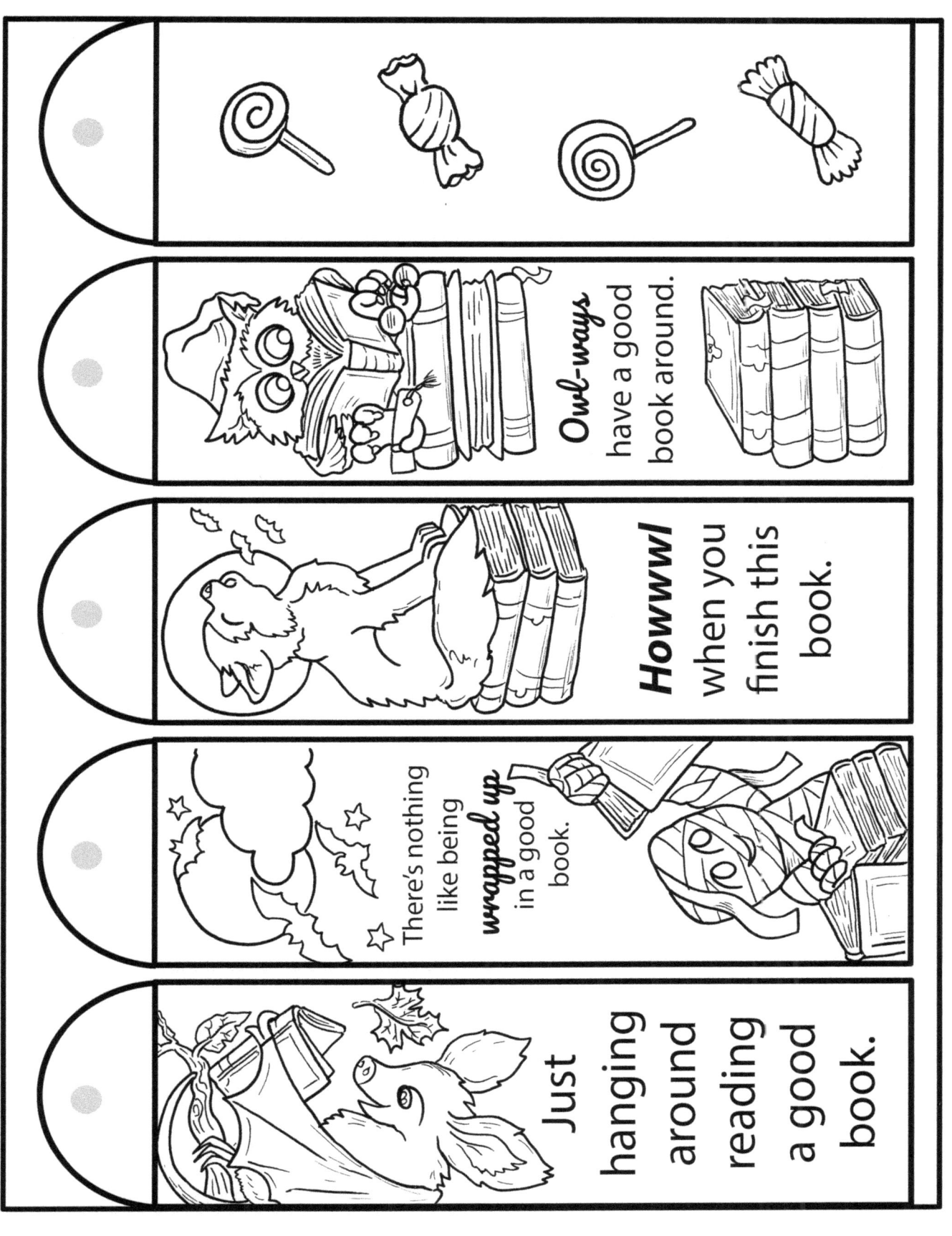

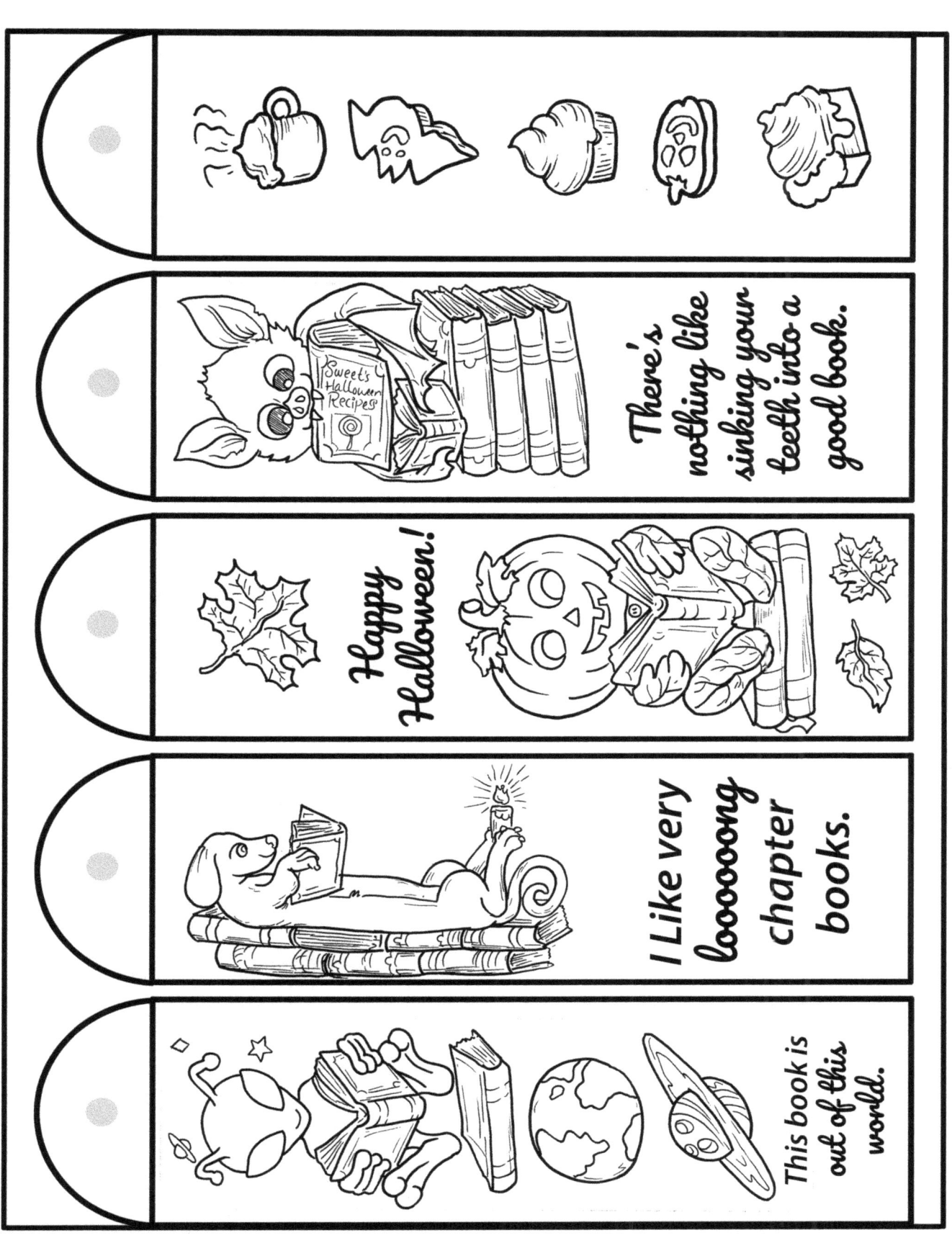

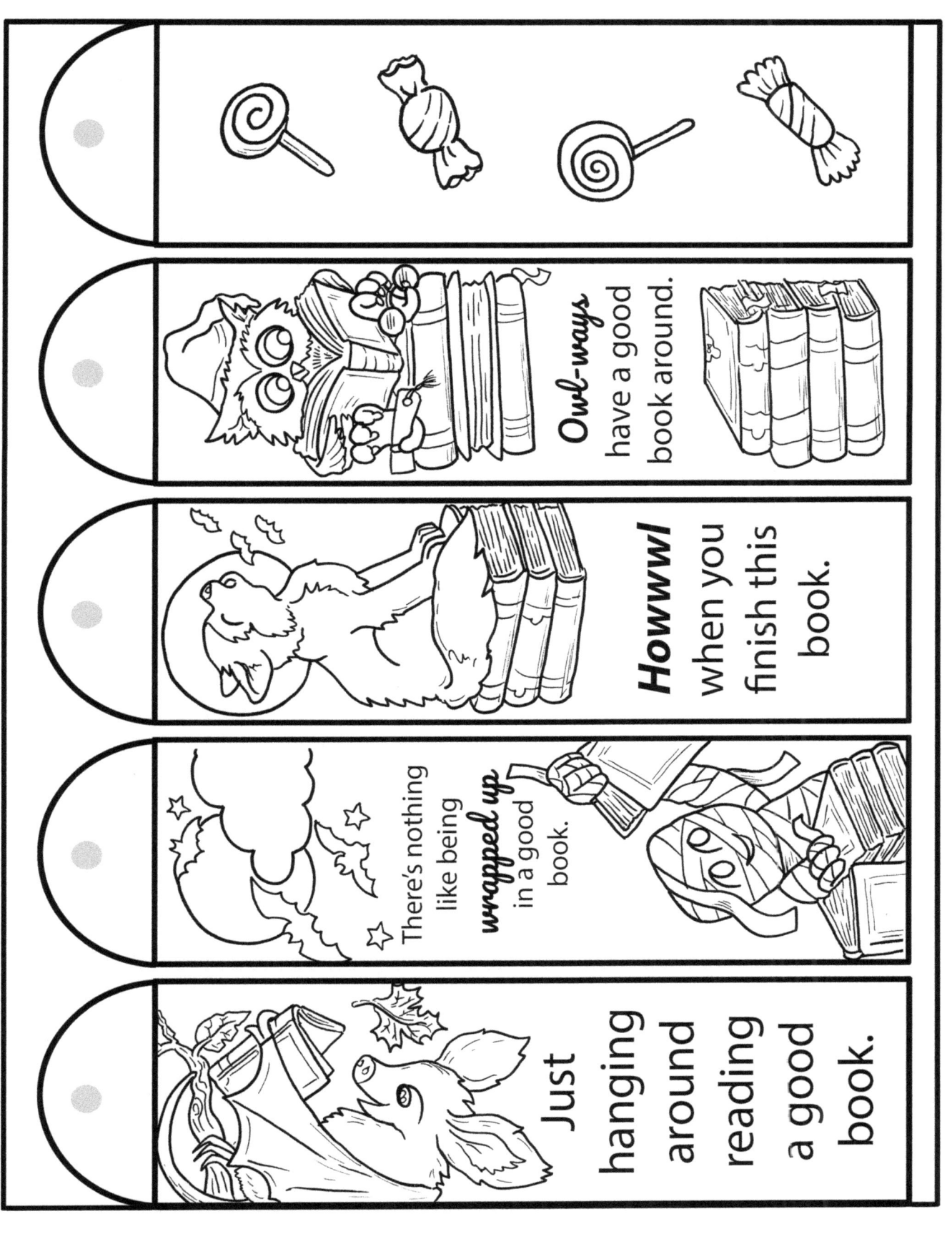

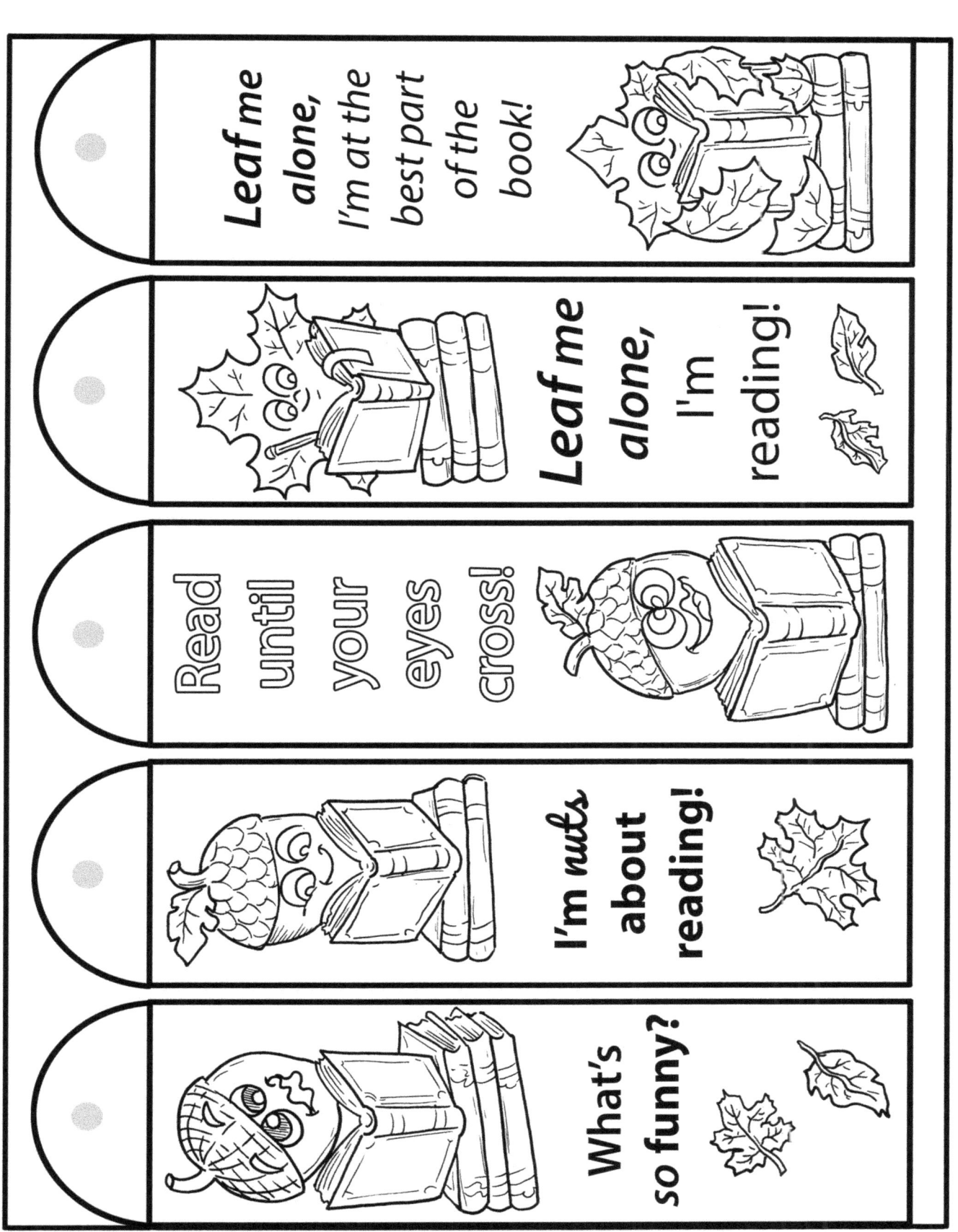

Bumblebee

Scientists recently found out that we **bumblebees** play for fun, just like you do! They saw us playing with little wooden beads in their laboratories. What toys do you think we like to play with in nature?

Do you know that our Queens **hibernate** underground in the winter? For Halloween, we prefer to collect pollen over candy. We help carry it from one plant to another, helping fill the world with all kinds of plants, including trees, vegetables, and flowers! That process is called **pollination**.

Did you know that some bees look like flies? Some of us make our nests underground. There are thousands of different kinds of bees in the world, but only eight of our species are honey bees. Yeah, we are unique, crucial and ***outstanding!***

The Domestic Cat

I am a **cat.** My eyes glow because of something called **tapetum lucidum**, pronounced tuh-pee-dum-loose-i-tum (like little mirrors in my eyes that reflect light). And we cats seldom meow at other cats. Maybe our meowing to humans is our version of speaking your language? We know of course, but won't say, because we enjoy being mysterious and strange; actually, our strangeness is thought to be one of our traits that had helped our survival in the wild.

Pin the Tail on Pumpkin Cat

Instructions:

1. Color in Pumpkin Cat and all 5 tails.

2. Cut out Pumpkin Cat and each of the 5 numbered tails. Cut along the dotted lines.

3. You can laminate Pumpkin Cat and all the tails in a laminator, or with packing tape to make them last longer.

4. You can decorate an envelope to save all your playing pieces for later. If you don't have an envelope, you can make one by stapling, or taping two pieces of paper together.

How to play:

Pin the Tail on Pumpkin Cat is a game you can play by yourself or with up to 4 other people.

You can play in two ways: on a tabletop or on a wall. To play on a wall, you will need tape or pins. To play on a tabletop, you won't need any tape or pins.

1. Set Pumpkin Cat on a tabletop or Pin or tape Pumpkin Cat onto a wall or pin board.

2. Give each player a tail, and a piece of tape to each person if you are playing on a wall so they can attach their tail to Pumpkin Cat.

3. The youngest player goes first. Either blindfold the player or have them squeeze their eyes shut tightly.

4. Each player takes a turn placing their tail where they think it should go.

5. Have fun playing!

Pin the Tail on Pumpkin Cat Examples:

These are some of the funny possibilities that can happen when playing:

Remove page, then cut along the dotted line.

Pin the Tail on Pumpkin Cat

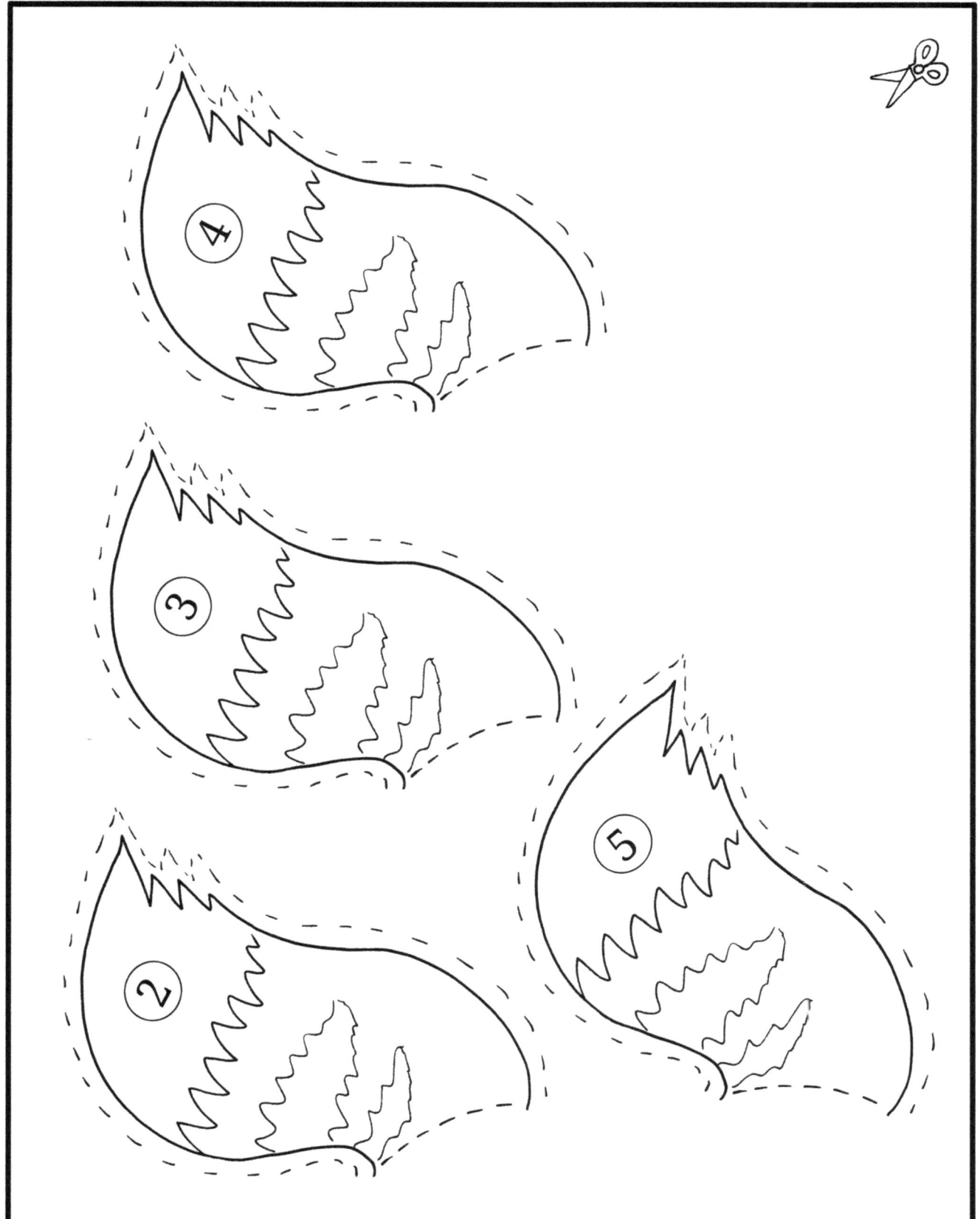

Color in the Pumpkin Cat playing page. Then cut along the dotted line to remove page.

Have a Bright & Happy Halloween!

Halloween
Trick or Treat Maze

Trick-or-Treat your way back to *Home Sweet Home,* but **be careful!**

Dog

The candies I'm eating are frozen peanut butter lollypops. I LOVE peanut butter (but I always check the ingredients to make sure there is **NO** Xylitol) it makes me sick!

I bet you know who I am? Yes, your very best friend of the animal kingdom, **the dog**. Unfortunately, as much as we'd like to, we dogs **can't** eat many kinds of human foods that you can eat. Many of our owners don't know some of the most dangerous foods that a dog should never eat. Here are some of them: **NO** chocolate or artificial sweeteners like xylitol. We can't eat onions, garlic, grapes, yeast dough, walnuts, or macadamia nuts. Please tell your family and friends so we don't get sick. And as much as I may beg, please don't share your Halloween candy with me. You can ask an adult to help you find treats that are safe for me, and I'd definitely like to munch on home-popped popcorn with you and watch Halloween movies!

Word Fill-In Game: The Halloween Cafe

Instructions: You can play this word game with family, friends, or by yourself. First, fill in the numbered blank spaces in the **Halloween Word Fill-In List** page with the type of word it asks you for, but don't look at the story page until you finish.

Next, fill in the numbered blank spaces on the **Menu at the Halloween Cafe** story page with the words from your word fill-in list. Lastly, read it out loud and have lots of fun!

To play the game, you will need to know what a noun, verb, and adjective is:

A **NOUN** is a word that names everything, a person, a place, or a thing. From the smallest to the biggest things that exist, from a planet to a pencil, from a bug to a galaxy, a noun is simply the names of everything and anything real or imaginary. A noun can even be a character from your favorite book or movie.

A **VERB** is a word that describes an action. Anything that a noun is doing is a verb. For example: run, jump, dance, sing, laugh, yell, read, sleep, eat, blink. Even to think or to stand still is an action!

An **ADJECTIVE** is a word that describes a noun. A noun can be: big, small, fuzzy, happy, energetic, grumpy, sweet, blue, messy, smooth, bumpy, beautiful, sour, smart, strange, funny, silly. Adjetives describe everything!

Word Fill-In Story:

A _____*BUMPY*_____ bat ordered a big bowl of _____*SOCKS*_____
     1. adjective   2. Noun
ice cream with ___*10,000*___ berries and ___*SINGING*___ - ___*CRICKETS*___ on it.
                     3. number   4. Verb ending in "ing"   5. insects of choice

Halloween Word-Fill In List

1. Adjective _____
2. Adjective _____
3. Adjective _____
4. Noun _____
5. Number _____
6. Verb ending in "ing" _____
7. Type of insect _____
8. Verb ending in "ing" _____
9. Type of candy _____
10. Noun _____
11. Yucky noun _____
12. Something stinky _____
13. Number _____
14. Icky noun _____
15. Type of dessert _____
16. Type of insect _____
17. Type of ice cream _____
18. Yucky word _____
19. Type of pie _____
20. Type of garbage _____
21. Least favorite dessert _____
22. Halloween animal _____
23. Type of insect _____
24. Least favorite vegetable _____
25. Yucky desert _____
26. Something disgusting _____
27. Body part plural _____
28. Number _____
29. Favorite candy _____
30. Adjective _____
31. Number _____

Menu at the Halloween Cafe

Welcome to the _____ Halloween Cafe where we serve the very
                1. Adjective
_____ foods in town! All our food is prepared by our world-renowned chef
  2. Adjective
_____ _____ Le'Sweet. We have _____ Halloween
  3. Adjective   4. Noun   5. Number
dishes on our menu.

TODAY'S SPECIALS

For starters, we have:

1. Cheezy Mozzerella _____ sticks.
                       6. Verb ending in "ing"

2. Deliciously steamed _____ pot stickers.
                    7. Type of insect

For the main course, you can pick between:

3. The charbroiled humongous _____ — _____ burger on
                          8. Verb ending in "ing"   9. Type of candy
your choice of freshly baked sesame _____ buns, whole
                                 10. Noun
grain _____ brioche, or organic sea salt _____ rye bread.
    11. Yucky noun   12. Something stinky

4. A heaping _____ cheese Pizza, topped with your choice of
             13. Number
_____, and _____, or _____ and _____.
 14. Icky noun   15. Type of dessert   16. Type of insect   17. Type of ice cream
Extra thin crust or double _____ stuffed crust pizza.
                            18. Yucky word

5. Howlingly delicious _____ spaghetti.
                     19. Type of pie

6. Deep fried _____ — _____ tacos.
       20. Type of garbage   21. Your least favortie desert

For a lighter meal, we have two farm-fresh options:

7. Fresh _____ droppings and bean sprout noodle soup.
     22. Halloween animal

8. _____, _____, and _____ salad with extra
 23. Type of insect 24. Least favorite vegetable   25. Yucky desert
_____. For dessert, we offer an extra large cup of _____
 26. Something disgusting   27. Body part plural
flavored hot cocoa, accompanied by a _____ foot platter of _____.
                                28. Number   29. Favorite candy
And finally, a great big slice of _____ pumpkin pie topped with
                             30. Adjective
_____ feet of whipped cream.
 31. Number

Enjoy!

Dolphin

Did you know we **Dolphins** are whales? Our cousins, the **Orca whales**, are the largest in our dolphin family. I bet you didn't know that only half of our brain sleeps at a time, while the other half remains alert, keeping watch for any danger. We also help sick or injured family members and have even been known to help humans in trouble. We have **two stomachs**, and we never chew our food! With our *two* stomachs, we'd be able to eat twice as much Halloween candy *if only our mothers would allow us to!* **Happy Halloween!**

Halloween Story Game: The Tour Guide is not Human!

Use your imagination to finish the story however you like, and draw a picture to go with it!

I won a ticket to swim with the dolphins in Hawaii on Halloween. When I got on the tour boat, I noticed there was something strange about the tour guide. I suddenly realized the tour guide was not a human, but a...

_____
_____
_____
_____
_____
_____
_____
_____

Halloween Story Game: The Tour Guide is not Human!

You can continue your story here:

_____

_____

_____

_____

_____

_____

_____

_____

_____

_____

_____

_____

_____

_____

_____

Frog

We frogs were the first known land animal that developed vocal cords. And believe it or not, we've roamed the earth since dinosaur times! Most frogs lay eggs in their environments, but the **Marsupial Frog** has a pouch like a kangaroo, where she keeps her eggs until they hatch. There are many kinds of strange and unusual frog species in my frog family, even one that can glide from tree to tree, called the **Costa Rican Flying Tree Frog**. Did you know that there is a frog called the **Hairy Frog**, nicknamed, the **Wolverine Frog**, that, as you can guess, looks hairy and can break its toe bones to reveal claws when in danger? Yes, sirree, that is me! My hair-like tissue helps me absorb more oxygen, similar to gills, so I can spend more time in the water protecting the eggs that Mother Frog just laid. Yes, we frogs are strange and amazing animals!

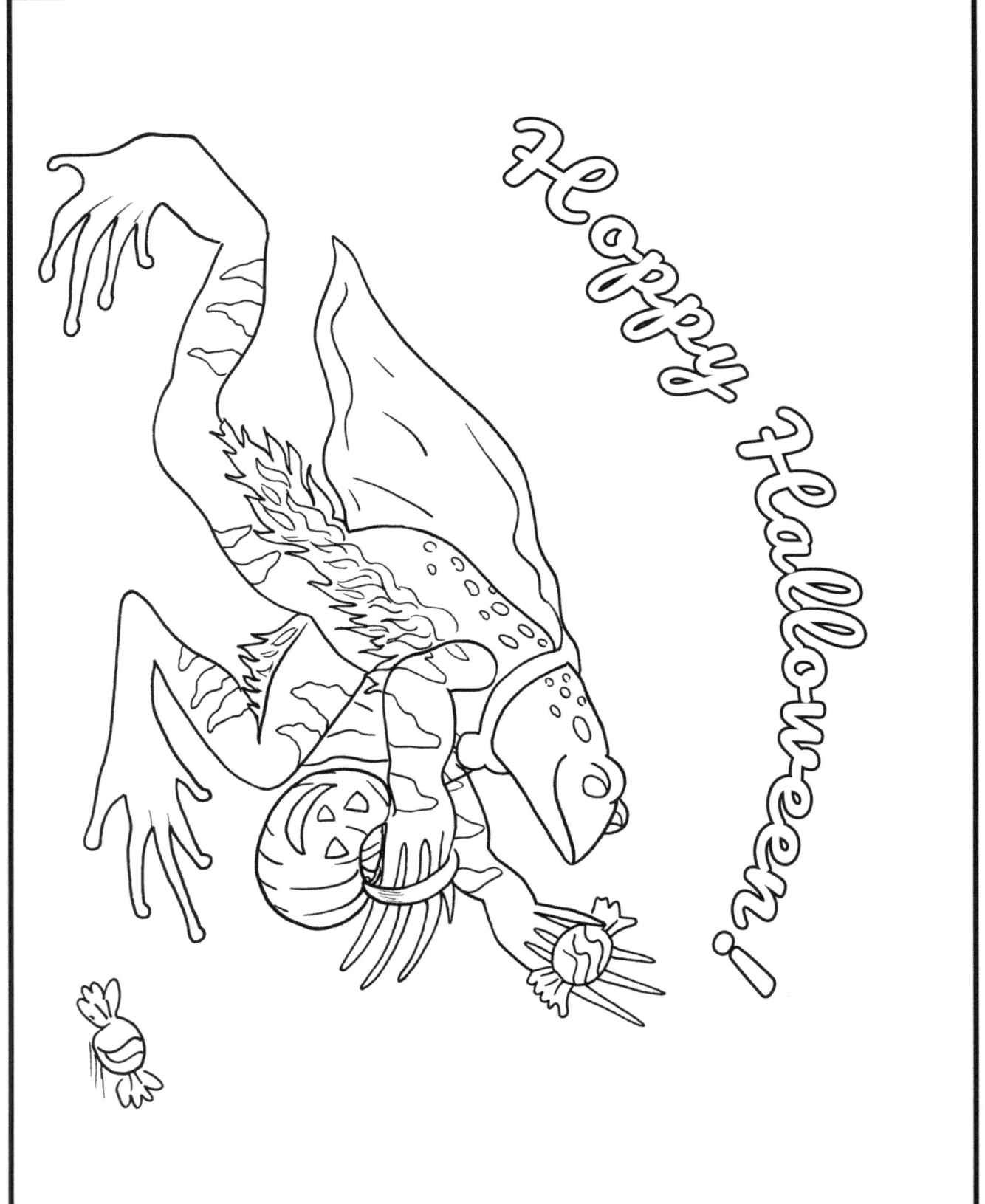

A Very Sweet Halloween!

The Pumpkin Daily Frog-News

EXTRA! EXTRA!
It's Halloween!

Toad

Believe it or not, a group of toads is called a knot! Many of our species produce poison from a gland on the back of our heads; one of the most poisonous toads in my family is called the cane toad. **Blinking is vital for us**, we need to blink when we swallow our food. Many people think we only make a loud croaking noise, but we make a unique array of sounds, from beautiful singing chirps to quacks, croaks, and hums. We breathe through our lungs like you do, but we also breathe through our skin. We toads take recycling to another level; when we shed our skin, we roll it up under our tongue and eat it! Leave no waste behind, we say! One last thing, ***don't touch us, we will scream in fright!***

Halloween Story Game: There's a Toad In The Kithen!

Use your imagination to finish the story however you like, and draw a picture to go with it!

In a much deeper voice than usual, you hear, ***"Breakfast is ready!"***
You scamper to the kitchen to see if there's something extra special for Halloween morning, but instead of a familiar face passing you your plate, a giant toad in a wizard's cap is roasting a marshmallow before your eyes, and then...

_____

_____

_____

_____

_____

_____

Halloween Story Game: There's a Toad In The Kithen!

You can continue your story here:

_____
_____
_____
_____
_____
_____
_____
_____
_____
_____
_____
_____
_____
_____
_____
_____

Manatee

We **Manatees** were mistaken for mermaids in the past, and our closest land relative is the elephant. Our larger cousin, the Sea Cow, is often mistaken for us. We can grow up to 13 feet long and I bet you didn't know that we were around with the dinosaurs! **We are very special.**

Maple Leaf

Deliciously sweet **maple syrup** comes from **maple tree** sap. A lot of work goes into making the syrup just right. To make one gallon of maple syrup, it takes about 40 gallons of sap!

Halloween Books and Movies

Write a list of your favorite autumn and Halloween books and movies:

_____

_____

_____

_____

_____

_____

_____

Grasshopper mouse

You can call me the **"Werewolf Mouse**," most people do, but my real name is the **Grasshopper Mouse of North America**, and I howl like a tiny wolf into the night. Yes, I'm super, but can you believe that I have adapted myself to no longer be affected by certain scorpion stings? Did you know that my cousin, the field mouse is monogamous (meaning when they find their true love, they stay together for life)? We mice may be small, but we are mighty *amazing!*

Star-Nosed Mole

I like forests, riverbanks, swamps, and marshes, and you can find me in North America. **I am the Star-Nosed Mole**, marked by my strange and special star-tentacle-shaped nose. I don't use it to smell with, instead, my **22 nose-feelers,** called **rays**, are more like fingers and eyes for finding and catching my delicious meals, like worms, bugs, and other small animals. I have more **sensory** "feeling" nerves and can eat faster than any other mammal! I could eat your Halloween candy faster than you could unwrap one chocolate bar! Luckily, I'd only go for your potato bug-pops or chocolate-covered crickets. There are a lot of other strange and interesting things about me, but I'd need much more room to tell you. ***Happy Halloween!***

Draw a funny face on the pumpkin.

Give your pumpkin a funny name:

_____

Halloween Tic-Tac-Toe

You can use pennies and nickles, or two kinds of candy, or you can cut out the pumpkin cookie and cupcake playing pieces from this page, and have fun!

Animal Mummies

Did you know that in **Ancient Egypt** people made animal mummies, including dogs, cats, bulls, hawks, birds, snakes, hippos, and crocodiles? Egyptians from that time were really *wrapped up* in making mummies*!*

Owl

We owls are amazing animals. We are very intelligent. Our babies are called owlets. When we are in a group, we are called a parliament, a wisdom, a stare, a congress, or a hooting, and we have three eyelids! There are over 200 species of us in the world, some are very unusual, but all of us are ***incredible.*** Our silent flight is admired throughout the animal kingdom.

Happy Halloween

Halloween Story Game: The Halloween Candy Mystery!

Use your imagination to finish the story however you like, and draw a picture to go with it.

You are looking through your Halloween candy when you find something incredible, it's a...

_____

_____

_____

_____

_____

_____

Halloween Story Game: The Halloween Candy Mystery!

You can continue your story here:

_____

_____

_____

_____

_____

_____

_____

_____

_____

_____

_____

_____

_____

_____

_____

_____

_____

OWl-ways Sweet

Reading OWL the time.

The Pig

We **pigs** are extremely smart, in fact, we are among the smartest animals on earth. Some people keep us as pets, and we can learn our names and other tricks in about two weeks. Some of us have learned to paint like artists, not only do we enjoy it, but we are among the best painters in the animal kingdom. Other animal friends, such as elephants, gorillas, the chimpanzee, horses, seals, sea lions, dogs, parrots, dolphins and beluga whales, have also learned to be amazing painters. Something else you may not know about us is that our mothers sing to us when we are babies, that we like to sleep nose to nose, that we don't sweat and that we have an excellent memory. Yes, you can say that we pigs are astounding!

Make a Pumpkin Masterpiece!

Draw a face on the pumpkin

Name your pumpkin:
_____

Pumpkin

Pumpkins originally came from Central America. Amazingly, they almost went extinct during the Ice Age.

Rats

We rats are a puzzle. Some people love us, some strongly dislike us. We've gotten a bad reputation in history, people thought that we carried infected fleas all over the world to spread a terrible sickness in the 1300's called the **bubonic plague**. Recent studies suggest fleas and lice from humans were the main cause of the spread. Good thing the record has finally been cleared! On a nicer note, some humans keep us as beloved pets, we are loyal and like to play. But, just as all animals, those who are wild, do not like to be pets, only rats from a pet store enjoy life with human companions. Contrary to popular belief, we are very clean. We are intelligent, and we care about our fellow family members. Did you know we laugh when we are tickled? Although, humans can't hear many of the sounds we make.

We need our whiskers to help us balance. And something many do not know is that we are an important animal on this planet, since we are an important food for many **animals of prey**, like owls, falcons, foxes, wolves, and more. And we are **pollinators**, we help spread seeds for plants to reproduce. We can be pests too, since we can chew through plastic, concrete, aluminum, and blocks of wood. We need to chew on things because our teeth never stop growing... So be careful with your Halloween candy. We love sweets! In fact, we love human food as much as you do! **Overall, we are smart and fascinating animals!**

Have a Bright & Happy Halloween!

Draw your Halloween sandwich:

Ingredients:

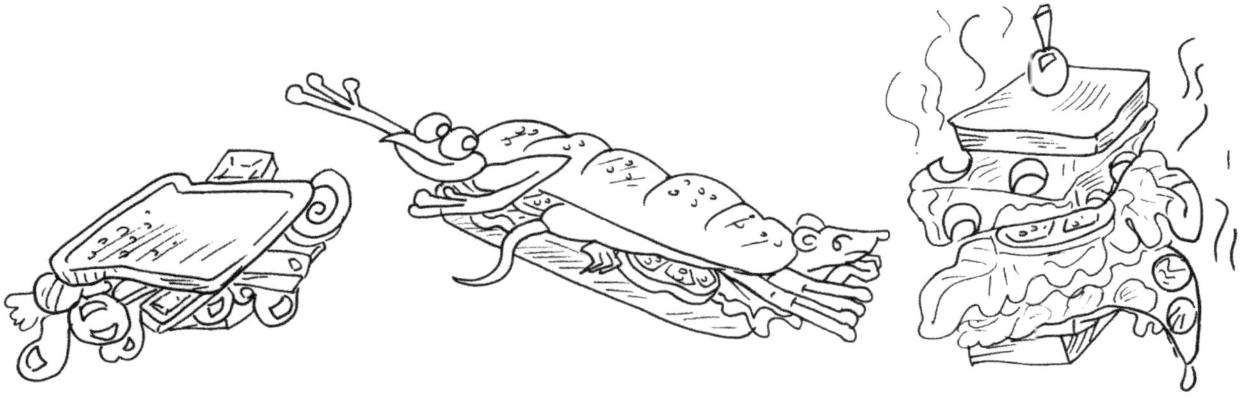

_____

_____

_____

Shark

We **Great White Sharks** are known as the biggest, toughest shark in the sea... But there's a lesser-known side to us. Although we are solitary, and keep to ourselves, we form friendships with one another, greet each other, and sometimes share our food. So, think of us when you share your Halloween candy! **Happy Halloween!**

Hammerhead Shark

Even though we **hammerhead sharks** are carnivores (meaning we eat other animals), some of us have seagrass in our diet, which, as you can guess, is unusual for a shark. We are also immune to the poison in stingray barbs.

Sailfish

We **Sailfish** have a special built-in heater to keep our eyes and brain warm in the cold ocean, just like our cousins in the Billfish family, the Marlins, Swordfish, and Spearfish. We are the fastest fish in the sea, and can swim 70 miles per hour. That's as fast as some cars go on the freeway! We have amazing colors, with dark blue at the top of our bodies, making a rainbow of blue-brown and silver tones towards our bellies. Did you know that some of us can change color instantly? From a deep glittery blue-purple-black, to a light blue with yellow stripes or splotches. When we are tired, we can turn a copper-brown color. We don't even need a Halloween costume!

Shrimp

We have our hearts in our heads. **'Opae 'ula** shrimp from Hawaii live up to twenty years old, and many people keep us as pets. Some of us help keep marine animals like sharks and fish free of bacteria, algae and parasites. One of our species, called the **Mantis shrimp**, can see far brighter colors than humans can!

Turtle

Some of us turtles can live up to 150 years or more. We have a soft-shelled cousin named, ***Pelodiscus sinensis*** (pe-lo-dis-cus sigh-nen-sis,) that urinates (pees) from its mouth! The tiniest of us are the ***mud*** and ***musk*** turtles which are the size of a candy bar. The largest turtles are called ***Leatherbacks*** and can grow up to seven feet long and weigh as much as 2000 pounds! We even had a thirteen-foot giant sea turtle ancestor named ***Archelon***, who lived alongside the dinosaurs!

My Favorite thing about Halloween:

Wolf

What is my favorite food? ***Howwwwlapeños***! Just kidding, we wolves are 100% **carnivores** (which means we eat meat). We are the largest of the **Canidae family** that we belong to, along with foxes, coyotes, jackals, dingoes, and the beloved domestic dog. Also, gray wolves are monogamous (meaning when we fall in love, we stay with our mate for our entire life, just like our cousins, the fox, coyote, and dingo). I would love to share your Halloween candy with you, but I'm afraid I'll be too busy ***Howwwwwling*** at the moon!

Happy Halloween

Howling Halloween Jokes

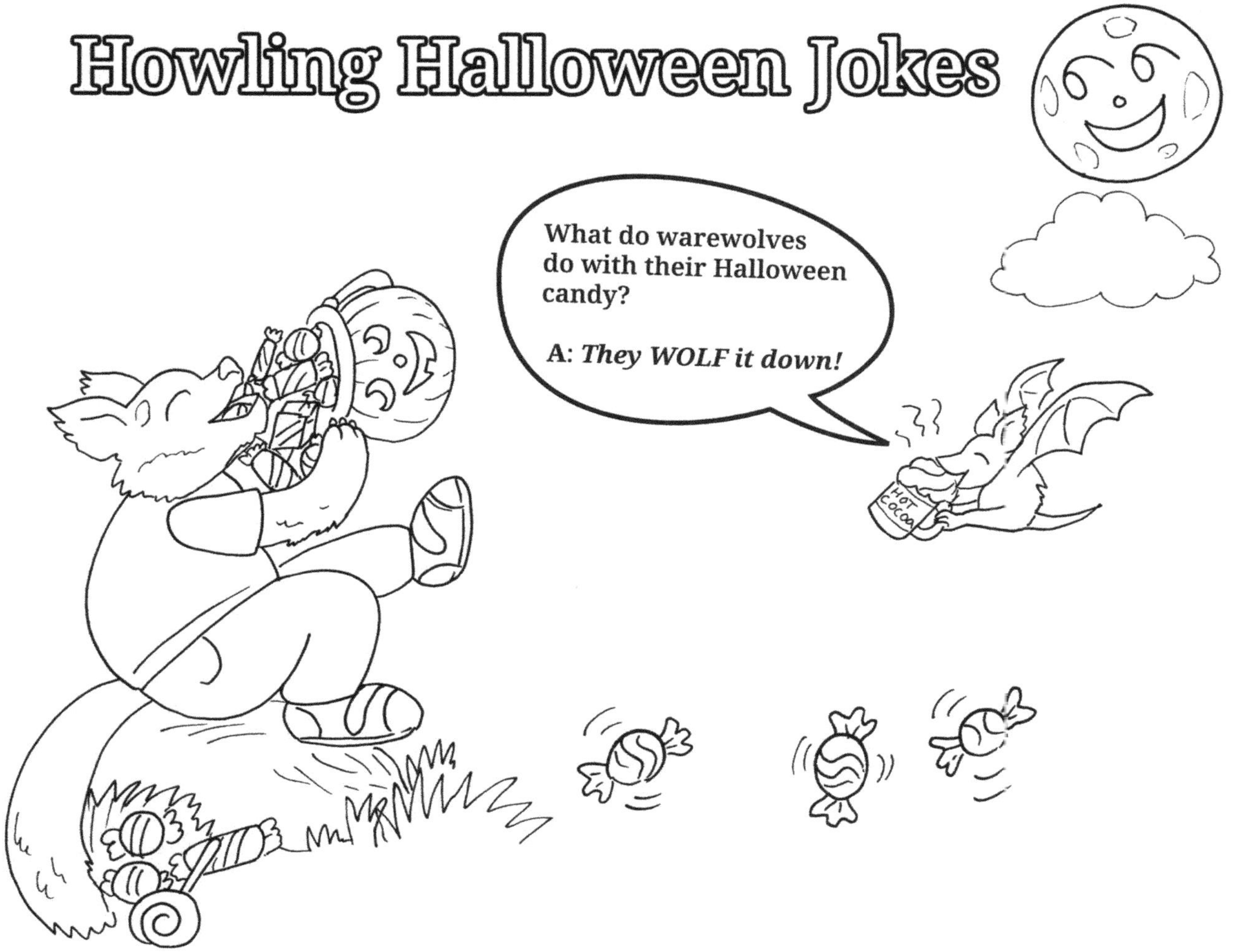

What do warewolves do with their Halloween candy?

A: *They WOLF it down!*

You can write some more *howlingly* funny Halloween jokes here:

_____

_____

_____

_____

_____

Halloween Paper Dolls

Instructions:

1. First **fully color** in the dog, cat, or pig Paper Dolls and their costumes. *Make sure to **finish coloring before cutting**, or the pieces can rip.

2. **Take out** the paper doll and costume pages, **one at a time**, and **carefully** cut them out.

*If it is too difficult, ask your parents or a grown-up to help you.

***Be extra careful not to cut off the tabs**. If you accidentally do, you can use tape to fix it.

3. Once all the pieces are colored in and cut out, fit the costume of choice on the doll and fold back the tabs to help it stay in place. If you need help seeing how the costumes should look, just look at the **"Halloween Paper Doll Examples"** on the next page.

*You can color and cut out the smaller **"Paper Doll Examples"** and **candies** if you want your own group of trick-or-treaters.

4. **Color** and take out one or all of the **Trick or Treat house** pages so you can take your paper dolls Trick-or-Treating from house to house.

5. You can save all the paper doll pieces in an **envelope or folder** when you are done playing. If you don't have an envelope, you can make your own by stapling or taping two pieces of paper together.

Most importantly, **have fun!**

Dog Paper Doll Examples

Here are the 7 dog costumes. You can dress your doll like the examples shown here or mix and match them however you like. Color and cut out the Halloween dogs and candy on this page for extra fun!

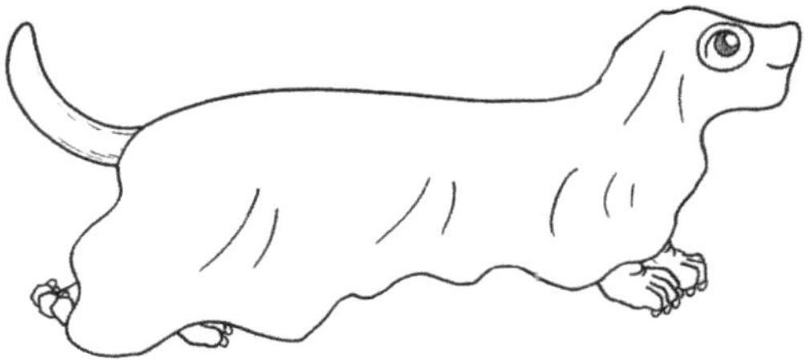

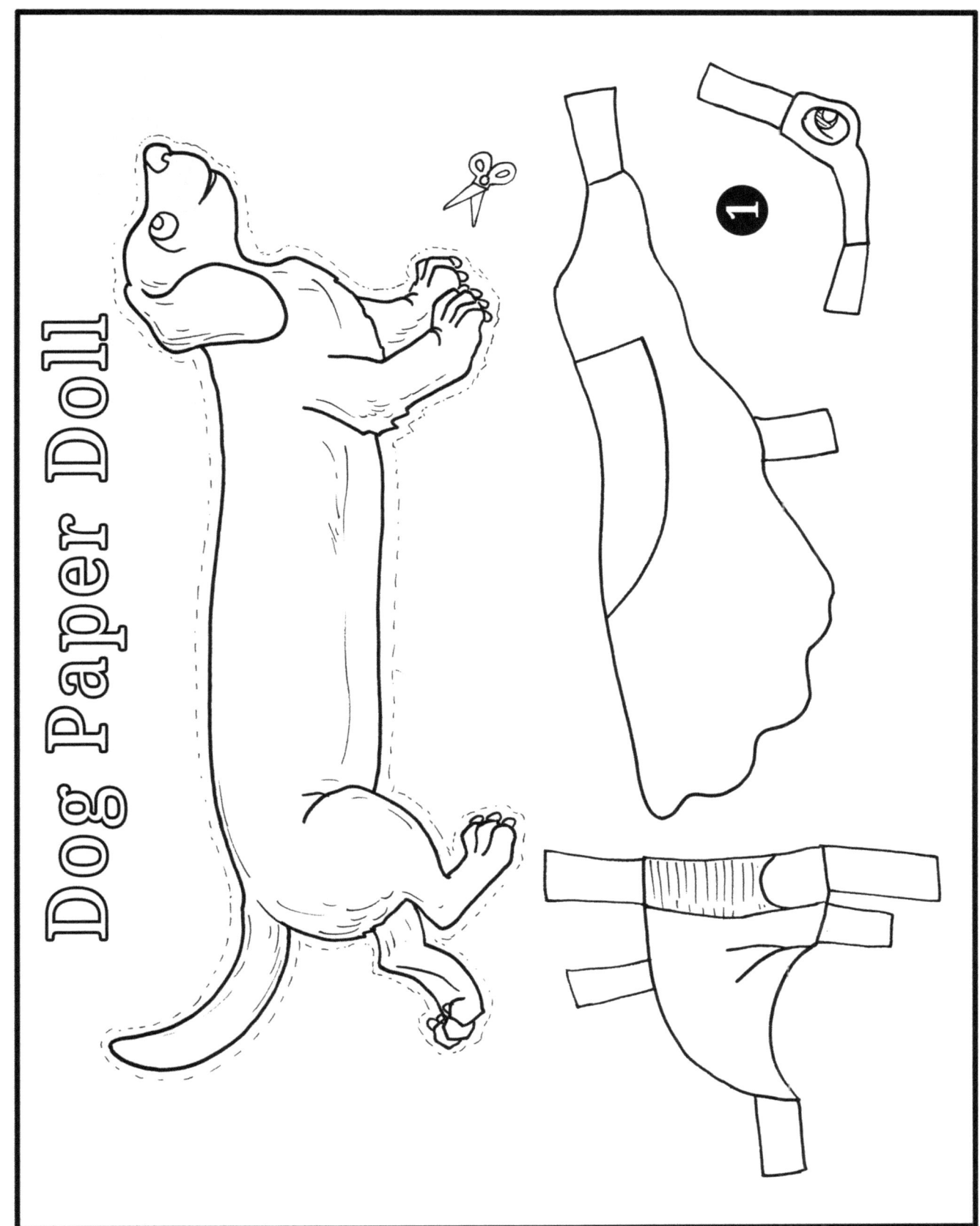

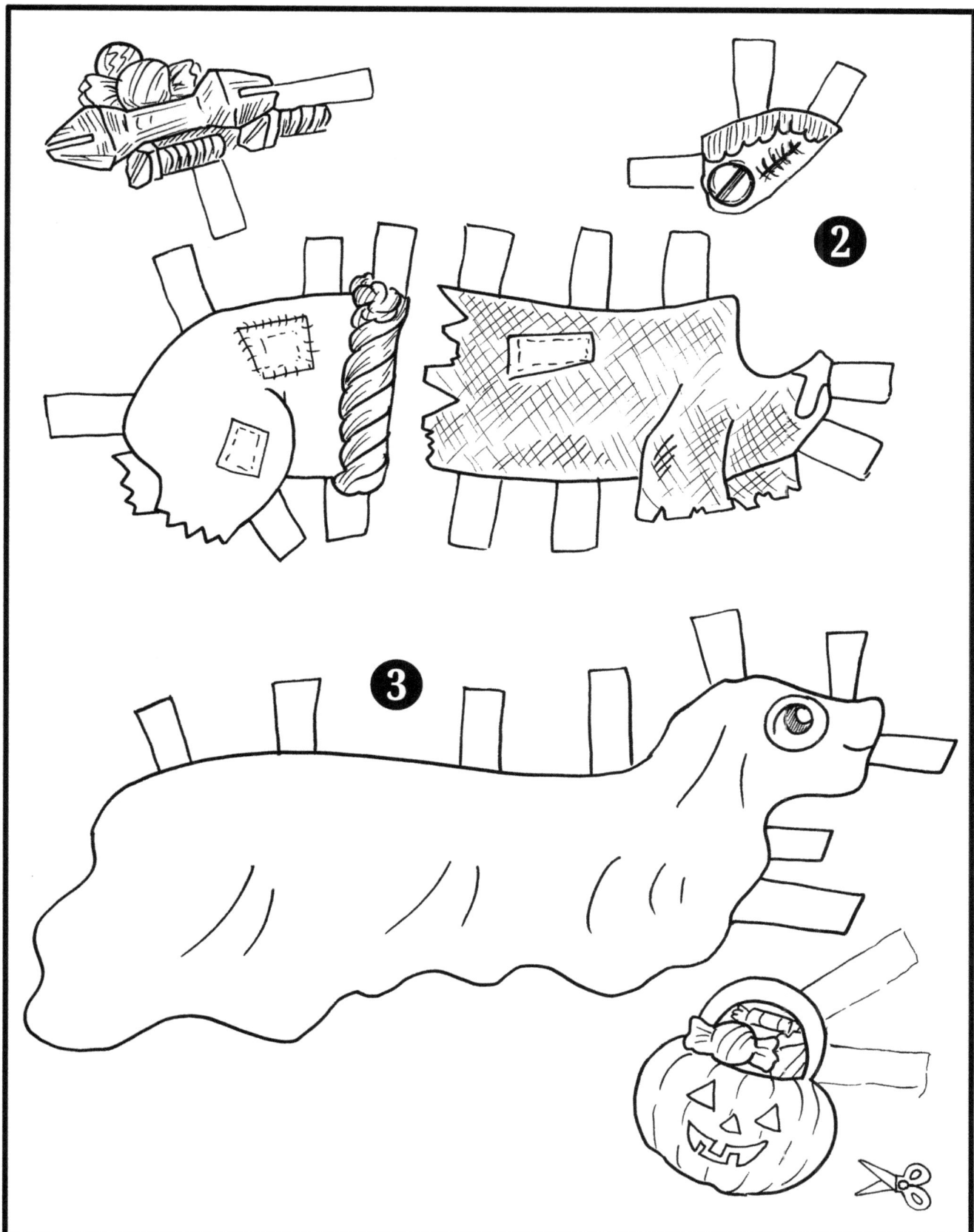

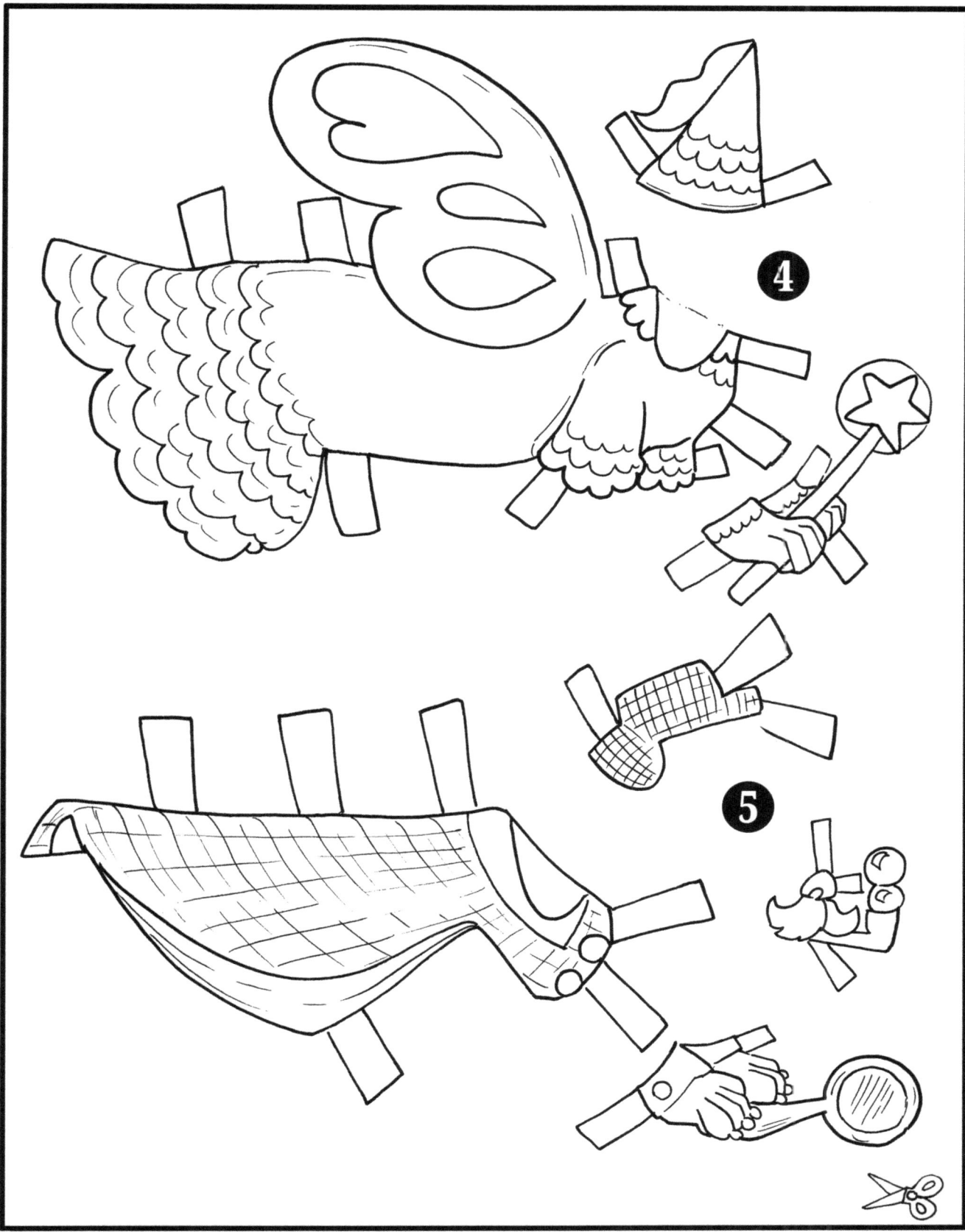

Cat Paper Doll Examples

Here are the costumes for your cat paper dolls.
There are 3 Little Cat costumes and 3 Big Cat costumes.

Little Cat & Big Cat Paper Dolls

Little Cat and costumes 1-3

Extra! Extra! Trick-or-Treating Candy!

Little Pig's Costume Examples

Here are Little Pig's four costumes. You can dress Little Pig like the examples shown here. The little piglets on this page can be colored in and cut out too, if you want some extra trick-or-treating piggies!

Little Pig Paper Doll

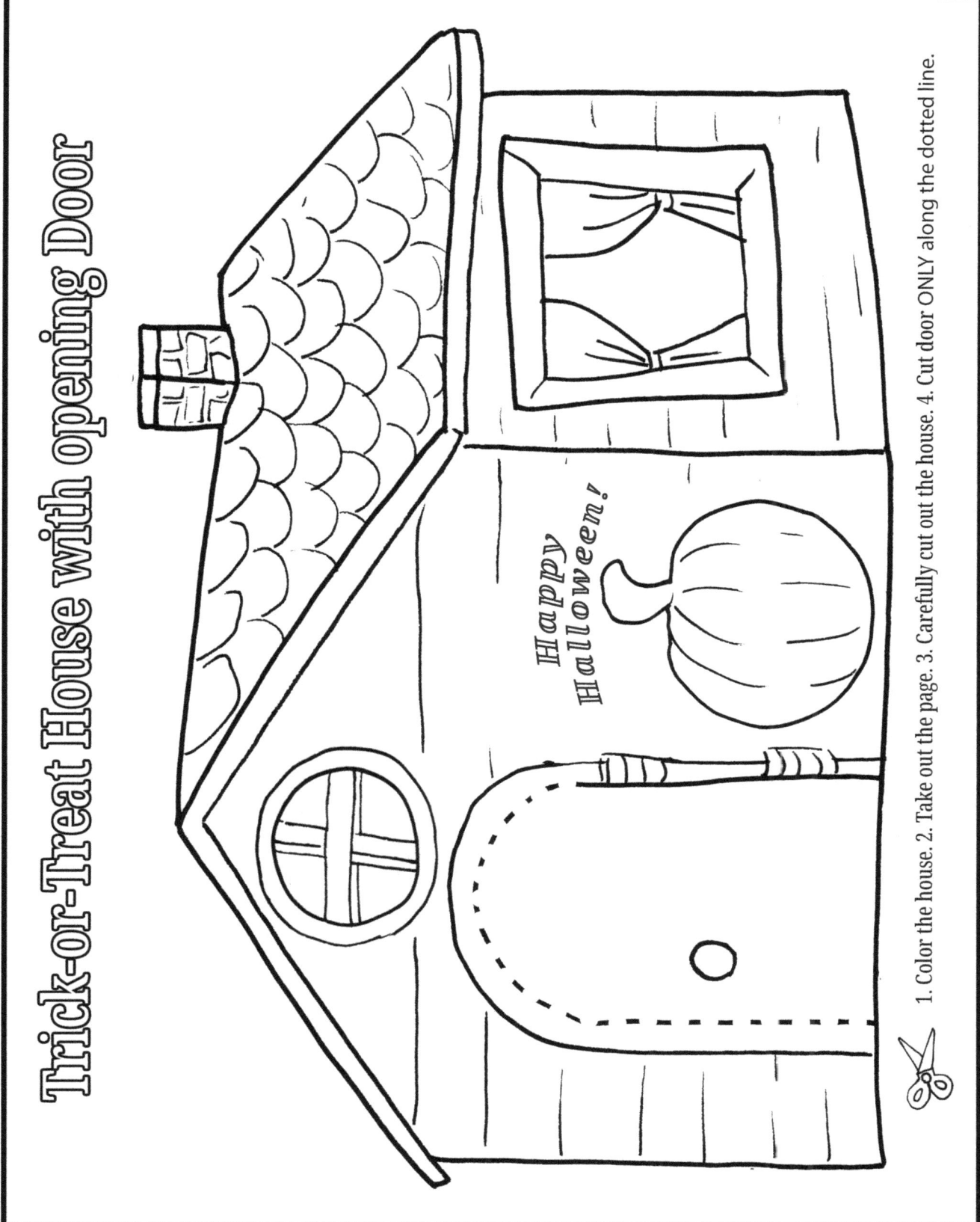

Paper Doll Trick-or-Treating Candy

Extra! Extra! Trick-or-Treating Candy!

Happy Halloween

Now, did you have lots of fun?
Then treat yourself to a nice candy and have a wonderful Halloween!

www.ingramcontent.com/pod-product-compliance
Lightning Source LLC
Chambersburg PA
CBHW061351010526
44107CB00011B/906